I hope you enjoyed this coloring book and that the quality and content exceeded your expectations.

If you did enjoy it, check out some of my other coloring books! They all have a similar style to this book and tend to have an outdoors theme.

Also, If you enjoyed this coloring book consider sharing a review on Amazon (it helps a lot!). Thanks once again for your support!

With appreciation,

Griffin R. Steele

Birds and Flowers Adult Coloring Book for Women 52 Designs (Includes: Hummingbirds, Cardinals, Sunflowers, Daisies, Roses, and More!)

ISBN: 979-8878033343

Charming Country Farm Coloring Book For Adults: Rural Landscapes That Include Countryside Farmhouse Scenes (52 Designs)

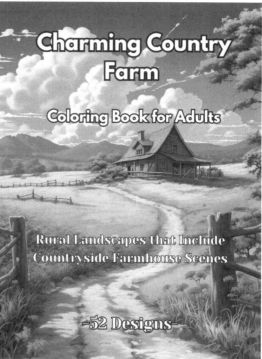

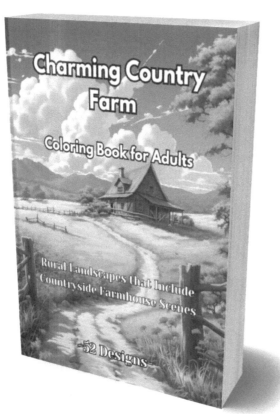

ISBN: 979-8878125055

"Whitetail Deer Adult Coloring Book with Wildlife Designs and Settings"

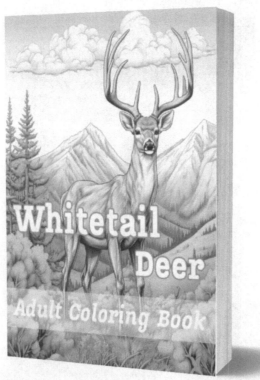

ISBN: 979-8872802563

"Fishing Adventure Coloring Book"

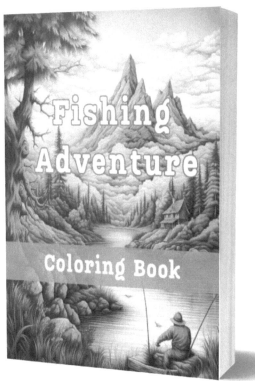

ISBN: 979-8870511092

Made in United States
Troutdale, OR
07/26/2024

21534987R10064